More Amazing
Quilted Photography ™

More Shapes, More Textures, & Many More Easy Techniques!

Tammie Bowser

Bowser Publications / Mosaic Quilt Studio South Pasadena, California

More Amazing
Quilted Photography ™

More Shapes. More Textures. ◦ Many More Easy Techniques!

Tammie Bowser

Editors: Sharon Hayes, Wally Taylor
Photography: Tammie Bowser
Book Design & Illustrations: Tammie Bowser

All quilts designed and made by Tammie Bowser except where indicated.

Attention Teachers:
Bowser Publications encourages you to use this book as a text for teaching. Contact us at www.QuiltedPhoto.com or at 626-799-5998 for more information about our teacher support program.

Library of Congress Cataloging in Publication Data
Bowser, Tammie
        Simply amazing quilted photography / Tammie Bowser
        ISBN 1-887467-51-3 (paper trade)
        1. Quilting. 2. Quilting--Art.
        3. Art.
        I. Title.

Published by:
        Mosaic Quilt Studio
        917 Fremont, PMB138
        South Pasadena, California 91030

Printed in the U.S.A.

Table Of Contents

Table Of Contents

Acknowledgments

Writing this second book has been a challenge. The challenge was how to describe and explain the creative possibilities with Quilted Photography. The creative ideas are coming to me faster than I can write! I want to thank God again for this endless source of ideas.

Thank you To my daughter Angela, for kissing me everyday. Thank you Ken for being a great Dad and for fathering Angela while I worked! Grandaddy, thank you for your encouragement. Thank you to all of my students, for inspiring me and sharing your photos and comments with me. Thank you Diana and Stephanie for helping me. Thank you mom again, for being my editor, and for being my biggest fan from the very beginning!

I could not have done it this second time without you all!

Tammie

"I have more ideas in my head than I could ever carry out....."

Vincent Van Gogh, May 1890

Preface

The goal of the this book is to teach you how to make Quilted Photos, and show you more ways to do it! This book is packed with new ideas. In fact there are new exciting concepts on just about every page. If you have my first book "Simply Amazing Quilted Photography", you may recognize a few illustrations from that book. Don't be fooled by that, the information is important and many times it has been modified to work with the new techniques. The first book's technique are not included in this book.

When you first look at the pictures of the finished Quilted Photos, your natural assumption will be that they are hard to make. The processes you will learn are easy, and also fast! The truth is, the processes are very easy to do if you take the time to understand each step, one at a time. Please read the book completely, and in sequence before starting your own Quilted Photo projects.

The ideas in this book are what I used to make the quilt on the front cover of this book. This quilt was a finalist in the competition "Quilts A World Of Beauty" at Houston Quilt Festival, 2003. I can not promise that your quilts will be finalists in Houston, but I promise that this book contains all the secrets I used for this quilt.

 Here is what one student wrote to me about her show winning quilt: "I found the Mosaic Quilt Studio on the web and was simply floored by the images and possibilities. The class was fantastic and I continue to work on photo quilts. The quilt I made in class has won "First Place" in two shows, one "Judges Choice" and one "Best of Show"!" Marlene Pearson
Santa Barbara, CA

"More Amazing Quilted Photography" can preserve your cherished family photos and transform them into works of art and if you really absorb the ideas in this book, you can be an artist yourself. This book does not have any patterns in it because the book includes a limited version of my software for you to download. This way you can choose your own Photographs and make your own patterns.

Thank you for your interest in "More Amazing Quilted Photography" and thank you for purchasing this book.

If you have any comments or questions that are not answered in the following instructions, please go to my website to ask me personally:
www.QuiltedPhoto.com

Art As Inspiration

In this chapter

I have respect for the work of the old masters like Vincent Van Gogh. I get ideas from the surreal artist Salvador Dali. I am also inspired by contemporary artists like Andy Warhol and Chuck Close. Each of these artists work is fantastic and differs from the other. I suggest that you look up each of these artists on the internet to see examples of their work. The more art you see, the more you will be influenced. With out any conscious effort, aspects of their works has pushed me to try new things. I have been influenced by all of them.

I will explain how the influence of each of these four artists has appeared in my newest "Quilted Photography" techniques.

Chuck Close

His work is amazing painted blocks of color. Blocks of color and value that together make a photographic image. Some of the work is painted in a grid formation, and others are in a grid that is turned on point! He is a really great contemporary artist that is still creating art today. I have used this same idea of turning the grid on point in my first book "Simply Amazing Quilted Photography" and I use this idea in this book as well. Read chapter 7 to learn how to turn your pattern on point.

Salvador Dali

This eccentric genius made a lot of outrageous art! Some of his work was sculpture and some were paintings, but all of them came from his unique point of view. I was captured by his portrait of Abraham Lincoln. From close up you see a lady looking into the sea, and as you back away, you see a portrait of Abraham Lincoln. The painting does not have thousands of blocks of color, it only has a few. This painting made me think about using less pieces of fabric. Using less numbers of pieces make the quilted image even more mysterious.

Before seeing the Abraham Lincoln painting, I thought that I would need thousands of pieces of fabric to create a photographic image. This understanding makes "Quilted Photography" something that is possible to make in a weekend!

Andy Warhol

The famous 70's pop artist, used color in a new interesting way. When I think about Andy Warhol, I think of his images of Jackie-O, Marilyn Monroe or Campbell's soup cans, all in bright color.

I have been using fabric to create things since I was three years old and I have a love for fabric and color. It is liberating to think that I can manipulate the colors in my "Quilted Photos" using all of the wonderful and colorful fabrics that are available. Manipulating the colors of an image brings surprising and dramatic results. Go to chapter 2 for the details of using color.

Vincent Van Gogh

Van Gogh uses spots of color to create images. I love his work and I sprinkled his quotes all the way through my first book.

My favorite quote of his is still this: "The best pictures, and, from a technical point of view, the most complete, seen from near by, are but patches of color side by side, and only make an effect at a certain distance" November 1885.

Van Gogh has a very famous painting called "Starry Night", not only does it have spots of color, but the spots of color have a swirling motion. I have made my own version of his painting "Sunflower", you can see his painting below and my version on my website. I used strips to create the movement in my version. Go to chapter 4 to see how to use strips to make motion in your own "Quilted Photos".

What Is Quilted Photography?

While studying graphic design, and computers I discovered that computerized photographs are not really photographs at all, they are just small squares of color that are arranged in a way that causes you to see an image. The more squares that are used to create the image, the clearer the image appears.

This concept works for fabric, tile or anything you can think of. It also works if the squares of color are dots, stars, triangles or any other shape. If you want to test this theory just find any book, newspaper or magazine, and examine a photograph with a magnifying glass. You will see small dots of color.

If you have already looked at the quilts in the gallery chapter, you probably are wondering why it is possible to use colors like blue, and purple and orange for a face? The colors are so unrealistic, yet the photograph is so real. Well that is because color value is much more important than just color alone. Color value is how light or dark a color is in relation to the other fabrics surrounding it. In chapter 2, I will show you how to sort your fabrics by color value. This special process will enable you to make a black and white image using colored fabrics!

Humans can see millions of colors, and most of the printed photographs you see in books, and magazines have hundreds of colors and shades in them. It would be a nightmare to manage a quilting project that has hundreds of different fabrics!

I have experimented with different numbers of fabrics. The number of fabrics that I have found to be manageable is 24. This number of fabrics will make your Quilted Photo projects beautiful, and intriguing!

The Quilts Look Painted

Next I will tell you what makes the new "Quilted Photos" look almost painted. Although the underlying concept of "Quilted Photography" is still to use a pattern of numbers as a guide for placing your fabrics,the techniques for putting the quilts together are very different than just piecing squares together. In this book I will teach you how to use other shapes, how to blur the lines and how to create texture. This may sound difficult, but as always, it is easy!

We will also be working with batik and hand dyed fabrics. These fabrics have a painted quality that will add a painted look to your quilted photo projects. Even though I will be focusing on batiks and hand dyed fabrics, other fabrics also work well. Since I already discussed printed fabrics in my first book, I will not repeat that

information here. I will instead tell you the important rules for choosing and using batiks and hand dyed fabrics.

9698531

With a single class, I was able to complete quilts with the unquestionable likeness of Rosa Parks and Rev. Martin Luther King Jr. They have been greeted with rave reviews. Who would have thought that a detailed portrait could be easily created by organizing fabrics and scraps. Following her simple rules, allows you to have tremendous results.
Sidney Hurd
Los Angeles, CA

Tammie, I did enjoy your class very much.. I was a little apprehensive at first, but the more I worked on it and then started sewing, it all came into place. My husband couldn't believe what he was seeing! Anyone that comes over keep asking "How did you do that?!"
Peggy Fullmer
Anaheim, CA

Value, Color, Fabric and Photographs

In this chapter

❖ Color Value Is The Key!
❖ The 888 Rule
❖ Two Extremely Easy Ways To Choose Colors
❖ Rules For Using Batiks & Hand Dyed Fabrics
❖ Choosing A Photograph To Quilt
❖ Taking Better Photographs
❖ Using The Color Wheel For Choosing Color

Read this chapter carefully because really understanding these concepts can be the difference between a stunning quilt or an average quilt.

Color Value Is The Key!

Color value is how light or dark a fabric is in relation to the other fabrics in your color palette. A color palette is the collection of fabrics used to make your

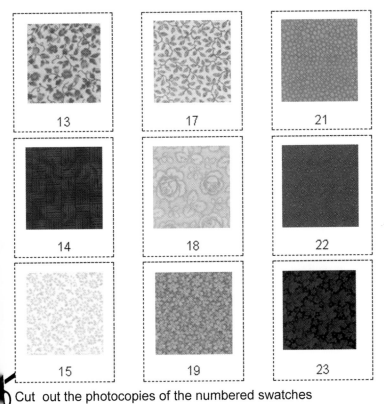

Cut out the photocopies of the numbered swatches

quilt. The most important step in making a photo quilt is arranging your 24 fabrics in order (from light to dark) by color value. I have found that it is hard for me to see the color value of fabrics with my naked eye. My eyes are easily fooled by the colors. To solve this problem, I use two processes that allows me to see the values of the fabrics separately from the colors.

Method 1

Cut a small piece of the fabrics you will be using to make your photo quilt. Photocopy the forms at the end of this chapter, then tape one fabric piece in each of the boxes. Make a black and white photocopy of the forms. IMPORTANT: The copy machine must capture grayscale. The photocopy will erase the colors, and only show you the value. Cut the photocopied swatches apart, and arrange them in order from light to dark. Now the values will be very easy to see. If two of your swatches look like they have the same color value, then make your decision about which fabric is lighter and which is darker by looking at the colors. You will use the numbers on the forms to identify the fabric order. Place your sorted swatches in a plastic organizer box

Method 2

For this method of finding the values of your fabrics, you will use the "Quilted Photo Xpress 1.0" software that you get by free download from my website. Just as in Method 1, you will cut a small piece of the fabrics you will be using to make your photo quilt. Use the form at the end of chapter 7, then tape one fabric piece in each of the boxes. Next you will scan the forms and open

Photocopied fabrics sorted by color value

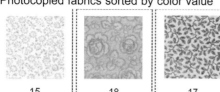 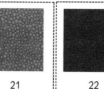

| 15 | 18 | 17 | 13 | 19 | 21 | 22 | 14 | 23 |

the file in the Quilted Photo Xpress 1.0 software and print your pattern. Your fabrics will be numbered and you will know if you are missing any values. Go to chapter 7 for the details for using the Quilted Photo Xpress software for this amazing method.

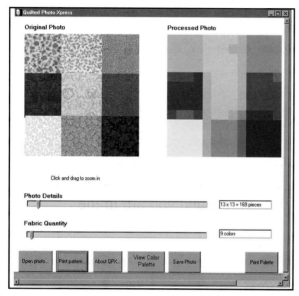

Once you have your fabrics in order by color value, your success is guaranteed! Not only is color value very important but it is even more important than the colors you choose! If you follow the previous instructions to sort your fabrics, you will effortlessly create highlights, shadows, and depth in your quilted photograph.

The 888 Rule

Another helpful guideline I use when choosing my fabrics is what I call the 8-8-8 Rule. You must have 8 light colored fabrics, 8 medium colored fabrics, and 8 dark colored fabrics.

Your goal is to have colored fabrics that represent shades from white to black. Don't be afraid to pick really light shades, as well as really dark shades because they are all necessary. You should be able to easily follow the 8-8-8 Rule while choosing your fabrics.

Do not worry about putting the fabrics in the exact order by color value yet, you'll be able to do that later, just concentrate on the 888 Rule while shopping.

A color palette is a collection of fabrics chosen for a quilted photo project. Choosing the colors for your quilted image is the most creative part of the whole process! Your quilted photograph will become art with your selection of colors.

While shopping for your fabric, you may choose any colors you like but your choices will determine the final look of your quilted photo. For example your quilt will have a sophisticated look if you choose muted colors or neutral shades as your color palette. If you select primary colors, or very bright colors, your quilt will have a lively, fun look.

A very important rule to keep in mind while choosing your colors is to stay in one color range. For example, if you have muted shades, choose muted shades for all of your fabrics. Or if you choose bright shades, then choose all bright shades because a fabric that is out of the color range will stand out unattractively.

There are several types of color palettes you can try for choosing your colors I will explain each of them.

Restricted color palette

A restricted color palette is a very restricted range of color. This range can have as few as 2 colors. For example you can use pink and purple. While choosing your fabrics, be sure to observe the 888 rule.

Random color palette

A random color palette is made up of fabrics of any color combination. Choosing your color palette at random is fun! I call a quilted photo made with a random color palette the ultimate scrap quilt! The random color palette is the most surprising type of palette. It really is hard to believe that putting 24 totally unrelated fabrics together can create a beautiful photographic quilt. You could even use all of your favorite fabrics, just be sure to follow the 888 Rule. Once you make a photo quilt with a random color palette, you will understand the importance of color value once and for all. You will not have to make any hard fabric selection decisions; you will only have the 8-8-8 Rule to remember.

Single color palette

A single color palette is made up of just one color, from the lightest to the darkest shades. This type of palette will work well with any image. It will be like making a colorized black and white photo. Just remember to follow the 888 Rule while choosing the single color palette.

Realistic color palette

A realistic color palette is made up of fabric that closely resemble the colors of the original photograph. Choosing the fabrics for a realistic color palette is the most challenging type of palette to put together. It is more challenging because you will have to consider the colors and values of the fabrics at the same time. This could mean you will have to shop around to find just the right fabrics to match the color palette.

To make your own patterns with realistic colors, you will need to upgrade to the 2.0 version of Quilted Photo Xpress software. I don't suggest you try a realistic color palette for your first project.

Two Extremely Easy Ways To Choose Colors

Choosing fabric seems to be the hardest part of the "Quilted Photography" project for my students. I know it can get confusing when you are in the middle of a quilting store surrounded by 1000's of fabric bolts! I have been thinking about this problem for the last year and I have come up with two surprisingly easy shortcuts that make choosing fabric less of a dilemma.

To use the first shortcut, start by choosing one fabric. Use the colors in the first fabric as a clue for choosing the next fabric. Keep choosing your fabrics with the last fabric as a clue for the next and your palette will have a wonderful, smooth transition from one fabric to the next. Remember the 888 rule.

For the second shortcut, go the thread section of your quilt store. Look at the beautiful variegated threads. You should see a beautiful assortment of cottons, rayons, polyesters and even metallics. They all can be a starting point for choosing your colors. You can use more than one type of thread, for example pick one dark and one light spool to use together on one project.Variegated threads have fantastic color combination that are already worked out for you, and as an added bonus, the thread will be perfect for quilting your project later!

Rules For Using Batiks And Hand Dyed Fabrics

I have begun to use batik and hand dyed fabrics because of the beautiful painted effect they give my quilts. You can try them too, but you must observe the following rules to be successful. I also use printed fabrics for my photo quilts,the details for using printed fabrics are discussed in my first book "Simply Amazing Quilted Photography". You can also go to my site to read about other options and tools for choosing fabrics and color.

Here are the three rules you must observe while choosing Batik and hand dyed fabrics.

Rule #1
Only use fabrics that have a consistent color value. If the hand dyed fabrics have more than one color, they must be in the same value family. For example if the fabric has light colors, all of the colors in the fabric must be in the light range of color.

Rule #2
Avoid tie dyed fabrics. They usually have big splotches of highly contrasting colors. Tie dyes are usually not suitable because the color value can change drastically from one area of the yardage to another.

Rule #3
Try to choose batiks that have a small pattern and that read as solids as much as possible.

Choosing A Photograph To Quilt

The first rule that must be considered while choosing a photo is the light balance. It is ideal to have a balanced photograph that is not to light, or to dark. If the light areas of the image are really light, or if the dark areas are excessively dark, you will not be able to see the details of the image. If the image has a minor imbalance, it can be adjusted, but if the image is far out of balance, your quilt will not have clear details.

Balanced Photograph

Light Photograph

Dark Photograph

Taking Better Photographs For Quilted Photography

Although I am not a photography expert, I do know what kind of photographs work best for Quilted Photography.

Digital cameras are so simple to use, and the processing time is cut down to cut down to almost zero. It is possible to make great photos for quilting, as long as you have the right instruction. After reading this section, you will be able to spot a good photo or a bad photo for Quilted Photography.

A great photo to use for Quilted Photography of a person or any other object has one light source. The light should come from one side, not from a flash on the top of the camera. A flash on the camera will shine a strong light right on the front of the face of a person, washing away all of the shadows, details, and contours.

A better way to create the right kind of light is to sit by a window. The light will shine in from one direction and you can see the results before you even take the photo. If the shadow is not dark enough, get a dark cardboard or piece of fabric and hold it on the side of the subject that the shadow should be. The darkness of the cardboard will absorb the extra light.

Another way to get great light is to go out side and use the early morning or the late afternoon sun. A good rule to follow is take your photos before 10am or after 2pm. The mid-day sun will wash away all of the shadows, details, and contours.

For each of these lighting tips, pay attention to how the light is shining on your subject, and move around until you like how the light is shining on your subject.

Remember that shadows and light are equally important. When you include both shadow and light in your photos the quilts will be well balanced and pleasing.

The photograph below is a good example of the light source coming from one side and it has interesting shadows. This photo made a beautiful quilt, and you can see it in the Gallery chapter.

Photocopy/Color Value Swatch Form

IMPORTANT NOTES: Copy must be grayscale so that you can see the values in varying shades of gray. First photocopy these forms, then attach your fabric swatches to the squares with tape or glue. Cut out the photocopied swatches. Arrange them in order by color value.

Attach Fabric
Swatch Here

13

Attach Fabric
Swatch Here

17

Attach Fabric
Swatch Here

21

Attach Fabric
Swatch Here

14

Attach Fabric
Swatch Here

18

Attach Fabric
Swatch Here

22

Attach Fabric
Swatch Here

15

Attach Fabric
Swatch Here

19

Attach Fabric
Swatch Here

23

Attach Fabric
Swatch Here

16

Attach Fabric
Swatch Here

20

Attach Fabric
Swatch Here

24

Using The Color Wheel For Choosing Color

The color wheel is a very useful tool if you know how to use it, and very confusing if you don't. I have come up with a few simple suggestion on how to use it for Quilted Photography. I have not seen these techniques any where else, so read carefully, it will help you.

This is a standard color wheel with primary colors , secondary colors and Intermediate colors.

Primary = Red, Yellow and Blue
Secondary = Violet, Green and Orange. This is a mixture of two primary colors.
Intermediate = The mixture of a primary and the adjacent secondary color

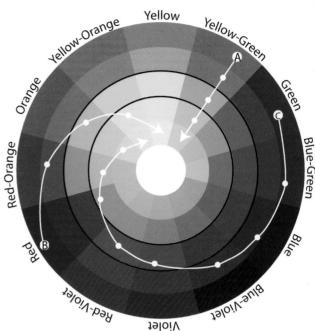

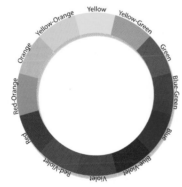

We are also concerned with the value of the fabrics you will use for Quilted Photography, so notice that the base colors in the color wheel is in the center, and the lighter and darker values are below and above it.

Try choosing your colors starting from the lighter pastels on the inner circle, moving out to the darker colors. I have marked some

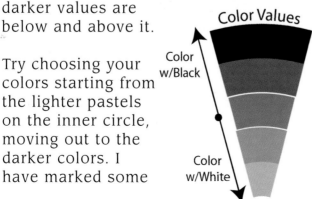

Color Values

Color w/Black

Color w/White

way to do this with the white arrows. You can move straight out, or curve around the wheel. It is OK to curve around clockwise, or counter clockwise. I always start with the warmer colors like yellow, orange or pink, but you can start anywhere on the wheel.

These colors are the example palettes for the above selections.

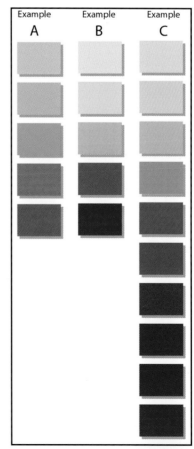

Example A	Example B	Example C

Gallery

Self Portrait

In this chapter, I want to show you some of the quilts that I have made with the techniques in this book. You will see that the possibilities are truly endless. I am always working on new quilts, and you can see more at my website.

This is a portrait of me. I have resisted for a long time, but I finally made myself with the stripy technique and I love it. The pattern was turned on point so that the strips look like a woven basket!

A Study Of Color

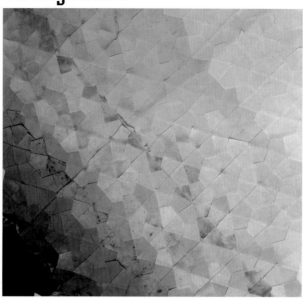

When I am working with new colors, I will sometimes try doing a small gradation. I do this before making a whole quilt so that I can see if I like it. For this particular study, I did not choose my colors well, if you look at the greens, they got lighter instead of darker..oops! I have included this to show you that I make mistakes too!

Sadie

Sadie is the beautiful golden retriever of one of my students! She made another quilt from this photograph, and this is the version of Sadie that I made. I used random pieces of fabric, and did wild free motion quilting. This is one of my favorites.

Quilting Detail

Kitty 1

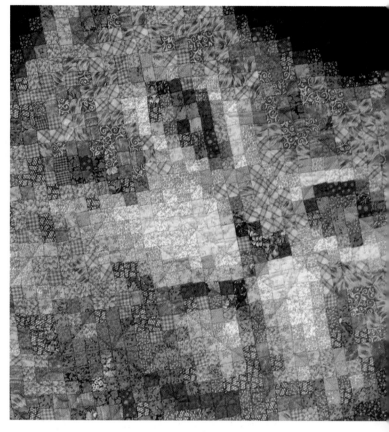

If you have seen my first book, then you have seen this kitty on the cover. I have gotten so many comments about it that I decided to make it again with a new technique. For the quilt on the next page I used 1/4" strips. I think I like it even better than the first one!

Kitty 2

Apple

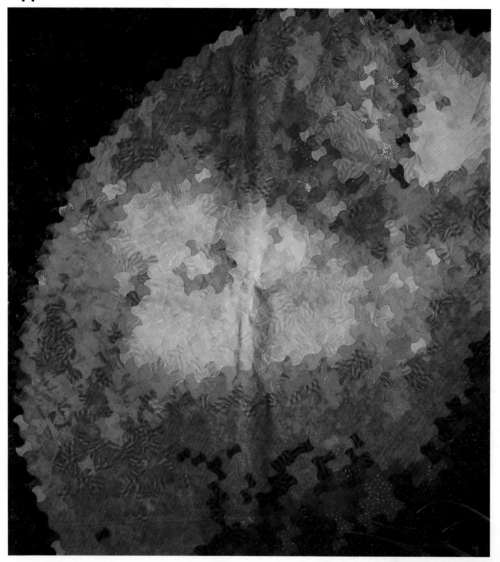

I made this apple with circles! I used a lot of red fabrics, and I layered the circles so that it would look like apple core shapes.

Baby

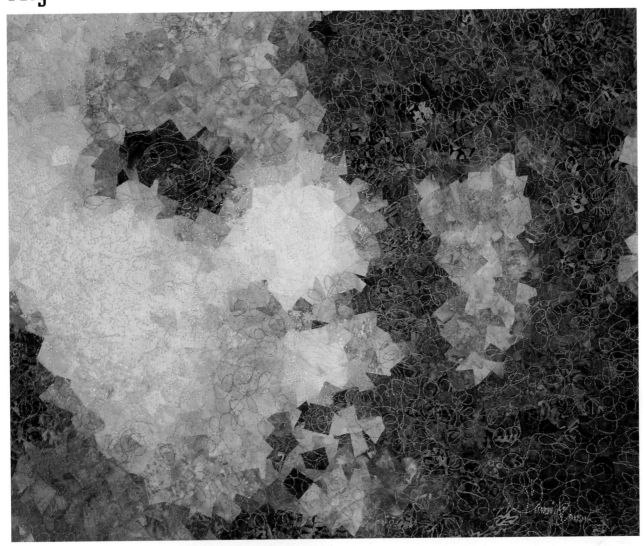

This baby photo is a good example of a good photograph to use for Quilted Photography. It has light coming from one source and the shadow makes the colors and contours in the quilt interesting. For the quilting I made very spontaneous, free motion loops.

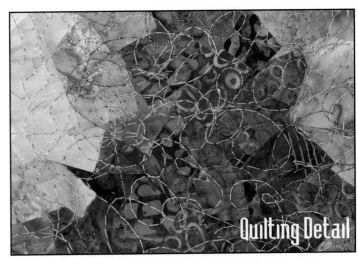

Quilting Detail

Uncle Jimmy

Quilting Detail

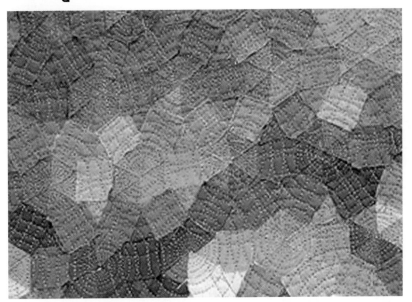

This photo is a portrait of my uncle in the 50s. I used solid colors that I dyed myself. For me the results were surprising and beautiful. I did the quilting with my Memorycraft 10000 embroidery machine, and I have included a close-up view of the stitching.

Unforgettable

This picture is of my grandmother Faye Evelyn Taylor as a 13 year old child. I have always loved looking at this picture and just had to make it into a Quilted Photo. This quilt has over 7000 pieces and is almost life sized. at 30" x "64". It feel like she is in the room when it is on display.

This quilt was entered and chosen as a finalist, in the competition "Quilts A World Of Beauty" in Houston 2003. I was proud to be chosen as a finalist.

My grandmother died a few years ago but I hope she sees the quilt and knows how much I love her still.

5 Dollar Bill

I made the 5 dollar bill with the random technique. I liked the first one out of squares, but this one is even more beautiful. The quilting is in gently curving lines in metallic thread to mirror the little lines in real money!.

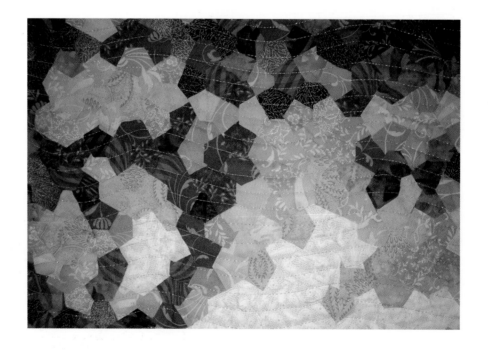

My Studio

Lots of you have asked about my studio, so here are couple of photos for you to see it.

It is a beautiful space with a lot of windows and a great view of Los Angeles. I can see downtown and the Hollywood sign at the same time!

Working here is very relaxing and most days I lose track of time and almost forget to go home. I do invite students to take classes in my studio, so if you are interested, go to my website to see my teaching schedule.

Tammie is a lovely, energetic & wildly creative woman! I thought quilted photography would be intense and difficult, but with amazing results.....only half of that is true, her technique is simple, clear and it does yield amazing results!
Alexis Durham
Manhattan Beach, CA

I found the Mosaic Quilt Studio on the web and was simply floored by the images and possibilities. The class was fantastic and I continue to work on photo quilts. The quilt I made in class has won "First Place" in two shows, one "Judges Choice" and one "Best of Show"!
Marlene Pearson
Santa Barbara, CA

reparing The Fabric Pieces

In this chapter

Overlapping Shapes

The techniques described in this chapter all involve overlapping fabric shapes that are fused and then quilted together. We will use squares, triangles, strips, circles or any shape you can think of. Using all of these new shapes is possible because the new techniques don't require any complicated piecing.

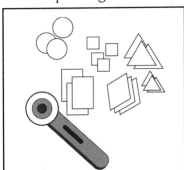

Fusing Options

After choosing your fabrics according to the rules in chapter 2, applying fusible webbing to back of the fabrics is the next step.

Fusible webbing is a heat activated adhesive that is applied to the back of your fabric so that it can be permanently adhered to another piece of fabric. All of the techniques in chapter 4 require fusible web on the back of the fabric.The fusing will allow you to fuse the pieces together,

creating a complicated looking, layered effect. I have found these fusing options for you to choose from.

Fusible Web - Regular fusible webbing is a fabric like material. It is applied to the back of fabric with a teflon coated ironing sheet. The teflon sheet will keep the fusible web fabric from fusing to the ironing board, or anything else. The fabric and the fusible web will peel right off. I have found a non-stick paper to cover my ironing board, and I use it over and over again to apply the fusible webbing to my fabrics.

Fusible Webbing Spray - Fusible webbing spray is a fantastic product! You simply spray the back of your fabrics, then let it dry for about 3 minutes, and that's it! You are ready to cut your fabric. I love this fusible webbing spray! Remember to follow the instruction for the correct iron temperature for this product. Go to chapter 8 for details.

Lite Steam A Seam 2 - Steam A Seam 2 is a fusible webbing with adhesive on both sides. This product is great if you don't want to use an iron while you are placing your pieces together or if children will be working on the project. To use it just peel the paper off one side, stick it to the fabric, then cut your shapes. You will peel the paper off the back of each shape when you are ready to stick the pieces together. Stick the fabric pieces according to the pattern.

Steam A Seam2 also comes on a roll, apply a strip from the roll directly on the interfacing, peel the paper and apply the fabrics by the numbers. After the pieces are all together, fuse them with the iron to make the bond permanent. Remember to follow the instruction for the correct iron temperature for this product.

Size And Scale

Now you must cut your fabric. The techniques described in this book can be made with very small pieces(1/4"), up to about 1"or bigger. Small pieces are possible because they are fused together....No Piecing! Since the shapes are overlapping, you **MUST** cut them bigger than the squares in the pattern as shown below. This rule is true for any shape you choose.

5	8	15
8	9	10
1	7	18

You can choose any size and/or shape you want. The size of the fabric pieces you decide to use will determine the final size of your quilt. The size of the pieces will determine how much fabric you will need. The size of the fabric pieces will also determine how far away from the quilt you will need to stand to see the image. With these things in mind, I do have a few recommendations to help you choose your size.

The size of the fabric pieces you use is very important. For example a quilt I made with 1" pieces finished 24"x40". The same quilt made with 1/2" pieces will only be 12"x20" and if it were made with 1 1/2" pieces, the quilt would be 36"x60". Notice how the size of the quilt changes with each different size piece.

The other thing you must consider while choosing the size is where the quilt will be displayed when it is finished. The size of the pieces will determine the distance that will be required to see the photo image. The bigger pieces require more distance, and the smaller shapes will need less distance. The magical beauty of these photo quilts is that when you look at the quilt from a distance you will see the photo very clearly, but as you get closer to the quilt, the image will disappear right before your eyes! When you are standing close to your quilt you will see a beautiful rainbow of fabrics, color and texture.

Fabric Cutting Tips

To cut geometric shapes like rectangles, squares, triangles and other scrappy shapes, I recommend that you use a rotary cutter, ruler and mat.These suggestions work perfectly with a regular straight blade but you should also consider trying a scalloped or other fancy blade or pinking shears as a wonderful variation. This will give your quilts another texture that you might enjoy. When you cut your fabric please use all the safety precautions and methods described by the manufacturers of the equipment.

I use a special ruler with a lip on the edge that makes cutting accurate shapes very easy. The lip guide keeps the ruler perfectly straight while cutting. I also use a handle on my ruler. The handle allows me to apply pressure to the layers of fabric. The applied pressure keeps the fabrics from moving while cutting. To learn about this special ruler and accessories, please go to my website or chapter 8 for more information.Note: I usually cut 1/16th of a yard of each fabric in my palette to begin with. If you start with more then that, you may have to much fabric leftover.

To Begin Your Cutting

1. First fold your fabric in half with the salvage edges of the fabric together as shown.

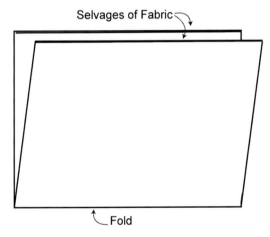

Selvages of Fabric

Fold

2. Now fold the fabric in half again matching the salvage edges to the folded edge.

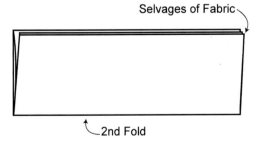

Selvages of Fabric

2nd Fold

3. Using your rotary cutter and mat, cut strips the width of your desired shape size. To make accurate strips, I use the guidelines on the cutting mat as well as the lines on the ruler.

4. Place the folded edge of the fabric on a guideline on the cutting mat as shown. Now if your ruler has a lip on the bottom, you will be able to slide it along the straight edge of the cutting mat to help you cut with accuracy. This process will go quickly once you get the hang of it.

Use a rotary cutter and mat to cut strips the width of your squares

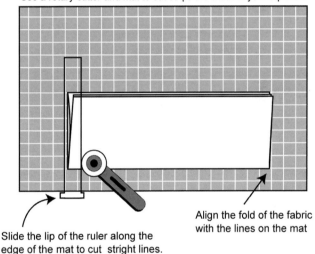

Slide the lip of the ruler along the edge of the mat to cut stright lines.

Align the fold of the fabric with the lines on the mat

5. To cut squares, place the strips horizontally on the cutting mat, following the lines of the cutting mat. Now slide the ruler along the bottom edge of the mat to cut your strips into squares.

Align the folds of the strips with the lines on the mat

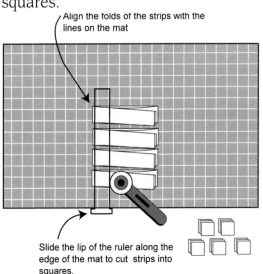

Slide the lip of the ruler along the edge of the mat to cut strips into squares.

Cutting Rectangles

Cutting rectangles is almost the same as cutting squares. Just cut the pieces with one side longer than the width of the strip.

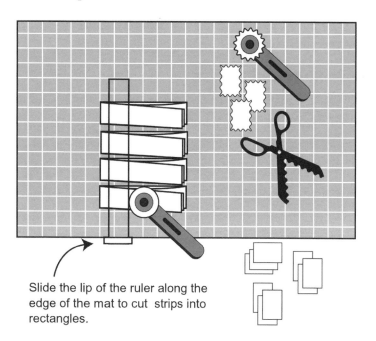

Slide the lip of the ruler along the edge of the mat to cut strips into rectangles.

Cutting Triangles

To make triangles, turn the ruler on opposite angles to create the shape. Don't worry about making a perfect triangle, it is not necessary to make a fantastic quilt.

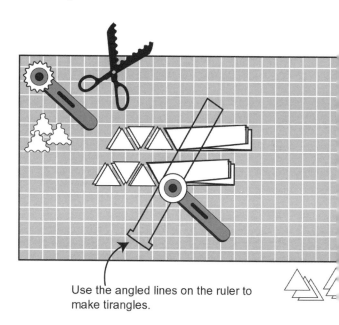

Use the angled lines on the ruler to make tirangles.

Cutting Diamonds

If you want to make diamonds, turn the ruler on an angle as shown in the diagram below.

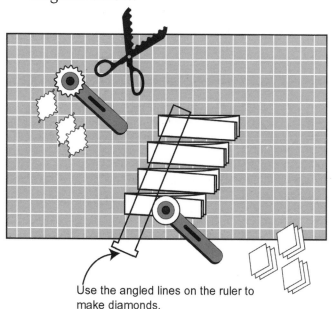

Use the angled lines on the ruler to make diamonds.

Cutting Circles and other Miscellaneous Shap

If you have not figured it out yet, you can use almost any shape you can cut. The shapes don't even have to be identical. Perfection in your cutting is not necessary and it won't even be noticed!

You can also use true scraps! Get rid of the ruler and just use your rotary cutter to cut up your fabric in any old shape.....it doesn't matter! Just be careful not to cut them to small. If you cut them to tiny, you will create extra work for yourself ....remember you still have to place each one of those tiny pieces.

If you want to try circles, visit your local fabric or craft store. They have circle cutters that will help you cut perfect circles. This process of cutting may take longer but the results will be fantastic.

Cutting Strips

Cutting strips are easy, and they are awesome! The strips can be any width you like and preparing them is very fast.The technique for using strips is exciting, read chapter 4 to learn more about it.

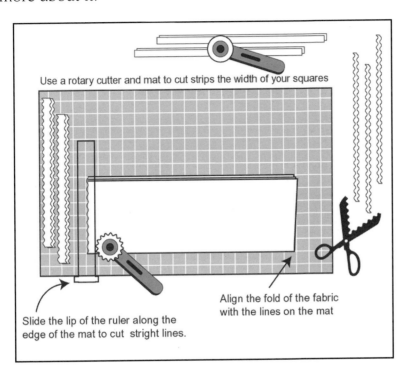

Use a rotary cutter and mat to cut strips the width of your squares

Align the fold of the fabric with the lines on the mat

Slide the lip of the ruler along the edge of the mat to cut stright lines.

Organizing Your Fabrics

After you have cut all your fabrics, make sure to place them in order from light to dark in your fabric organizer. Then number them from 1-24 with #1 being the lightest color. This organizer box will prevent you from losing any swatches, and it will also keep the fabrics labeled. To label the compartments, just use a permanent marker to write the number directly in each of the spaces or little labels work well too.

What if I run out of a fabric?
If you miscalculate your yardage needs and run out of a fabric you can substitute with another fabric. Since the quilt has so many fabrics no one will ever notice the substitution. The rule for substituting fabrics is, it has to have a color value that is darker than the fabric before it, and lighter in value than the fabric after it.

I've gotten many, many compliments on my quilted photo from women who have quilted far longer than I have! It is so much fun watching the images appear almost like magic!
Alexis Durham
Manhattan Beach, CA

I love the look of quilted photograph - it makes for a very personal quilt, one that people can't believe I made. People look at it and say "Hey, I see it, Wow that's great".
Dianne Langewisch
Pasadena, CA

mazing Quilted Photography Techniques

In this chapter

How To Read The Patterns

If you look at the sample pattern at the end of this chapter, the pattern information is stored in a grid. Read chapter 7 to learn how to use the software to make patterns from your own photos.

You have three options for using the numbered patterns. 1) purchase gridded, fusible interfacing to lay out fabric swatches, 2) use a paper grid guide to place under your plain fusible interfacing,(read chapter 8) or 3) draw your own grid guide with a large sheet of paper and a pen. You'll learn more about Grid Guides later in this chapter.

About Fusible Interfacings

Fusible interfacing is a very thin kind of fabric that has an adhesive on one side. The adhesive is activated when heat is applied with an iron. You will use the fusible interfacing to hold all of your fabric swatches in place. Technically you don't have to use fusible interfacing because your prepared fabrics will have a fusible webbing applied to the back. However I still use the fusible interfacing to make double sure my fabrics stay put!

The worst thing that could happen is for your fabrics to fall apart........ It is your choice.

Gridded Fusible Interfacing

This is fusible interfacing with a grid printed directly on one side. You can purchase gridded fusible interfacings at your local fabric store or quilt shop. The gridded fusible interfacing comes in panels, or running yardage that is either 44/45" or 60" wide. The most common grid sizes are 1", 1 ½", and 2". You can use any of these grid sizes, but re-read "Size and Scale" on page 34 before you decide what size to use.

Before using any of the gridded interfacings, read the manufacturer's instructions very carefully. The adhesives that are used are sensitive and may not stick well if the instructions are not followed correctly. As a general rule I suggest that you test out the interfacing before you place all of the fabric swatches. You can test the fusible interfacing by ironing a fabric swatch to a small piece of the interfacing. You should use the iron setting you intend to use for your quilt project. Let the swatch and interfacing cool, then try to pull the swatch away from the interfacing to check if the adhesive is working well. If the swatch comes off easily, try it again at a different heat setting.

You can also use any plain lightweight non-woven fusible interfacing, but you will have to read the manufacturer's instructions very carefully before using.

Plain Fusible Tricot

I use plain fusible tricot for all of my photo quilts. To use the plain fusible tricot, you must also use a grid guide with it (see chapter 8). I have tested several and the best kind does not stretch much, you can see through it, it is applied with a dry iron, and has an adhesive that keeps the fabric swatches attached securely. I have made this special fusible tricot available at my website and at the back of the book.

What Is A Grid Guide?

It is a printed grid that you place under the plain fusible tricot or interfacing as a guide for placement of your fabric swatches. The grid is printed on paper and you can use it again and again. The lightweight tricot that is used to make photo quilts are so thin that you can easily see the guide through it. Also as an added bonus, you can transfer the pattern information directly to the grid guide with pencil, then erase and use it again. Just be sure to use a pencil with soft lead so that your numbers will erase easily.

Note: you can also transfer the pattern information to the gridded fusible interfacing but be careful to use a pen or pencil that will not stain your fabrics when you apply the iron.

I prefer to use more than one grid guide at a time. I just tape several grid guides together to make one big guide, then I write my numbers as shown in the next diagram. These guides are the perfect tools for using with the pattern on page 47 or other photo quilt projects you will make later with the free software.

You can make you own grid guides too. You will just need a pen, ruler and

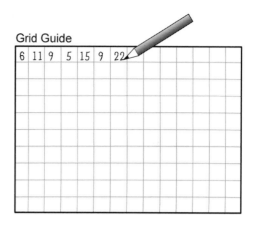

Grid Guide

| 6 | 11 | 9 | 5 | 15 | 9 | 22 |

paper. The advantage to this is you can customize it for your own preferences. You will be able to choose any grid size, and you can make a guide that will fit your work surface perfectly. Be very careful to draw accurate grid lines.

Place your grid guide on your work surface, then place the fusible interfacing **sticky side up** on top of your grid guide. This is very important so I will say it again...**the adhesive side of the interfacing should be facing up, towards you!**

You will be able to see the grid and the numbers through the interfacing.

Place grid guide on the table

8	4	2	4	9	5	3	9	3	2	11	4	3	4
5	8	4	2	4	9	5	3	9	3	2	11	4	3
4	2	4	9	5	3	9	3	2	11	4	3	1	1
8	4	2	4	9	5	3	9	3	2	11	4	3	4
5	8	4	2	4	9	5	3	9	3	2	11	4	3
4	2	4	9	5	3	9	3	2	11	4	3	1	1
8	4	2	4	9	5	3	9	3	2	11	4	3	4
5	8	4	2	4	9	5	3	9	3	2	11	4	3
4	2	4	9	5	3	9	3	2	11	4	3	1	1
8	4	2	4	9	5	3	9	3	2	11	4	3	4

Place fusible interfacing on top of the grid guide

lacing The Pieces

Placing the fabric swatches is really fun because you will start to see the image emerge as you place more and more pieces.

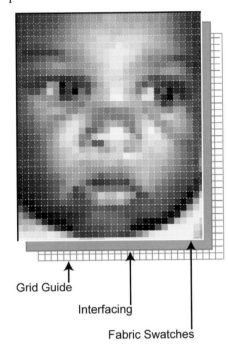

Grid Guide

Interfacing

Fabric Swatches

Transfer the numbers from your pattern to your grid guides. Start placing your swatches on the interfacing following the numbers and your chosen technique. (Keep reading to learn about the techniques).Look at the diagram above to understand how to position the grid guide, fusible tricot, and fabric pieces. You will see your photo image very soon!

Continue placing your fabric pieces until the pattern is complete. It usually takes me about 2-3 hours to put all of the swatches in place. This time depends on the amount of pieces and the technique you choose for your quilted photo.

A good tool to use is a small craft iron. This kind of iron is readily available at craft and quilting stores. This little

iron will give you control while placing your small fabric pieces. You can also use a regular iron.

After you finish the whole image, you should move the quilt top to an ironing board to make sure all of the pieces are fused well. The correct way to iron the swatches is to pick the iron straight up, then put is straight down. Never slide the iron around on the surface of the quilt top before the swatches are secured. Try to avoid letting the hot iron touch the bare interfacing. Continue pressing a section at a time until the whole quilt top is fused in place.

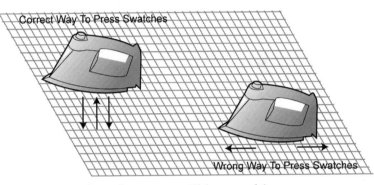

Correct Way To Press Swatches

Wrong Way To Press Swatches

Remember that you will be working very close to your quilt and the images are best viewed at a distance. For every one of the quilts that I have made, I think to myself "It Didn't Work This Time!". I have to remember to step away from it or look at it though a Distance Viewer. The Distance Viewer is like a small telescope that will enable you to see the quilt picture immediately. After the swatches are all in place, look at them through the Distance Viewer to see if you like the image.

If you want to make any changes this is your last chance to do so. To make the change, fuse a new swatch right on top of the old one.

Pixilated But Twisted

The first technique is called pixilated but twisted. You place the squares by the numbers, but you can twist the way the squares are placed on the grid. When the Quilted Photo is finished, it has a very random, painted look....but it's not! I have created these illustrations to explain the technique to you more clearly. The patterns that you will use for all of the techniques are a grid of numbers.

2	2	8	15	11	7
2	2	9	10	20	3
7	2	7	18	11	3
2	1	9	21	11	4
9	5	2	20	11	7
2	5	9	15	11	7

The first step for the Pixilated but Twisted technique is to start placing the squares. Some of them can follow the grid lines as shown.

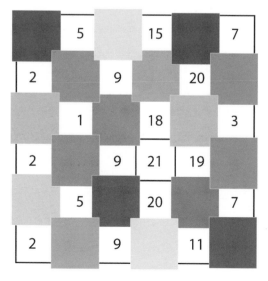

You will continue placing squares, twisting them however you want.Remember that you should have cut your fabric pieces a little bigger than pattern squares. Since the fabric pieces are bigger than the pattern squares, it is very easy to completely cover the surface and not have any open spaces.

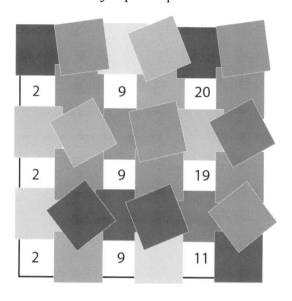

Now you will continue placing the squares until the surface is completely covered. The photo will look layered and complex....it will look beautiful and painted!

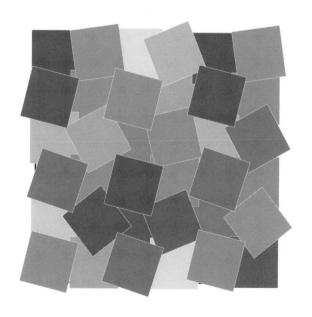

andom Shapes And Sizes

For the second technique, you can use different shapes and sizes of fabric pieces all in the same quilt. You will still need to cover the whole surface of the pattern but the pieces can be different sizes, shapes and of a different scale all in the same project. The pieces can be smaller than the squares of the pattern as shown here. You can even twist them, or not twist them as shown in this illustration.

		8	15	11	7
		9	10	20	3
7		7	18		3
	1	9	21		4
9	5	2	20		7
2	5	9	15		7

For the my next example I have completed the sample with big squares. The purpose of this example is to teach you that the fabric pieces don't have to be

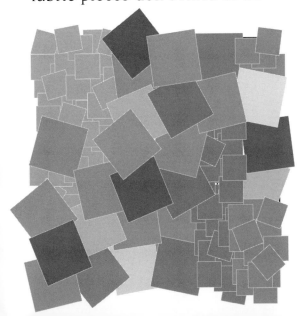

identical in size or placement.

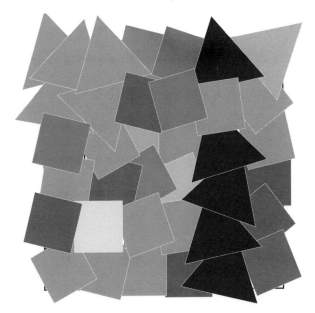

This last example shows that the fabric pieces can vary in their shape as well. I've used triangles and squares together.

Stripy

The third technique uses strips. Instead of having a separate piece for each square in the pattern, you will apply a strip along a row if the numbers are matching as shown below.

2	2	20	15	11	7
2	2	20	10	20	4
2	2	20	18	11	4
2	2	5	5	5	4
2	2	2	20	11	7
2	2	2	15	11	7

It is easiest to apply the strip if you use a small iron to fuse the end then cut the strip to the desired length. You continue with this process until the entire surface is covered.

I love the look of the strips technique, look in the gallery chapter to see examples of real quilts made with strips. Another variation the stripy technique is to try cutting your strips with scalloped edge scissors.

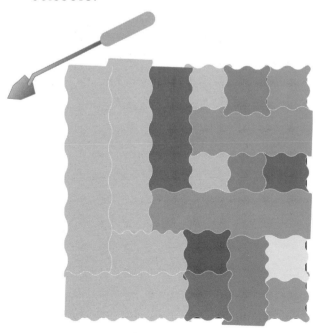

Bonus Variation

For the previous examples, I placed the strips according to the numbers at random, but another way to add interest is to create a pattern in the direction of the strip placement! I know this is wild....but it is fantastic! Try these patterns for strip placement.

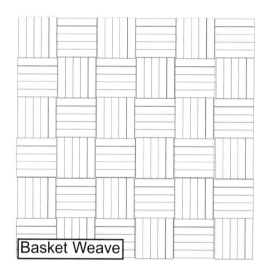

Basket Weave

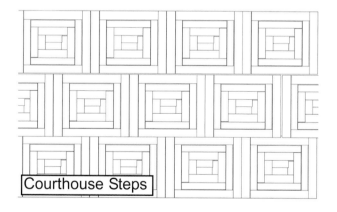

Courthouse Steps

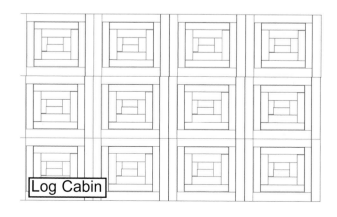

Log Cabin

Sample Quilted Photo Pattern

1	41
2	36
3	68
4	102
5	67
6	75
7	30
8	57
9	18
10	50
11	11
12	27
13	59
14	17
15	51
16	18
17	53
18	52
19	49
20	8
21	21
22	43
23	36
24	151

```
23 23 19 19 17 21 22 19 18 19 19 19 19 21 23 | 24 22 21 19 19 17 13 13 17 17 17
18 18 22 19 19 23 19 17 17 21 19 19 17 18 22 | 22 22 21 17 18 18 15 15 15 17 15
19 17 18  8 18 22 19 19 17 18 19 15 13 13 18 | 19 19 19 19 19 19 18 17 15 15 13
23 22 17 10 18 23 19 17 17 19 17 12 10 10 13 | 15 15 16 13 13 17 19 18 17 15 13
21 19 12 16 21 21 18 17 17 17 13 10  6  6  6 |  8 15 13  6  6  8 15 18 17 15 13
24 24 22 22 21 21 15 15 15 17 15  8  6  4  4 |  6 10 12  6  4  5 11 17 13 15 15
24 24 23 18 17 13  8 10 15 19 13  8  7  6  4 |  6 12 12  6  3  3  5 16 13 13  8
24 24 22 18 15 13 13 10 16 18 12  6  4  3  3 |  6 12 11  7  3  2  2  7 10 13 10
24 23 18 19 13 10 12 13 15 12  8  6  4  4  2 |  2  5  7  5  2  2  1  4  6 10 13
22 19 13 11  8  6  8 13 10  7  7  7  4  4  6 |  1  2  5  5  5  2  1  4  5 10 13
22 12  7  8  6  4  8 10  8  7  6  5  4  3 10 |  2  2  3  7  6  3  2  6  5  7 12
18  6  4 15  6  4  8 10  6  5  4  6  6  3  6 |  3  4  3  6  8  3  3  4  4  6 10
 8  4  8 17  8  6  8  6  5  7  5 11 12  9  6 |  5  4  3  4  6  3  5  7 18 18 10
 6  6 17 15  8  8  8  5  5  9 18 22 12 22 16 |  4  5  4  3  6  3  6 11 18  9  8
 5 12 19 13  8  8  8  4  4  3  4 14 19 23 22 |  3  7  4  3  5  4  6 14  9  4  8
 6 13 17 13 10 10  8  5  3  4  7  9  3  3 14 | 14  5  4  3  6  5  7  5  7  7  8
 6  8 17 17 13 10  8  4  4  4 11  9  5  7    |  9  8  4  3  8  5  8  7  8 10
 6  6 15 15 13 13 10  6  6  4  5  6  7  7  9 |  9  7  4  3  3  4  3  4 11 10 10
 6  6 13 15 13 13 10  6  4  4  4  5  7  9  9 |  7  5  3  3  4  3  4  4  6 12 10
 6  6 13 15 10 15 10  6  4  4  5  4  4  6  5 |  5  5  2  3  4  4  3  3  3 12 13
 6  6 10 18 13 15 10  6  4  4  4  4  3  4  5 |  7  4  4  4  5  4  4  4  3  8 15
 6  6  8 17 15 15 15 10  6  4  3  2  3  2  4 |  5  4  5  6  5  4  4  4  3  5 16
 4  8  8 15 15 15 17 15  8  4  2  2  3  3  3 |  3  6  6  7  5  5  4  4  4  4 16
 6 12  8 15 15 15 18 13 10  6  4  3  2  4    |  4  5  6  5  5  4  3  4  3 11
 6 12  8 17 15 17 19 17 13  5  4  4  2  4  4 |  4  4  9  3  3  4  4  4  3  7
 8  7  8 18 15 17 22 19 18 12  4  4  3  4  4 |  5  3 14 22 14 18 14  9 11 14 11
12 16 10 17 15 17 22 22 22 18  5  2  2  3  3 |  4  4  2 14 24 24 24 23 22 14  5
13 21 12 17 15 17 21 24 22 12  5  2  2  2  1 |  3  3  5 14 24 24 11  1  5
14 22 18 18 16 17 21 24 23 16  9  2  3  1  2 |  3  3  3  1  1  1 20 11  1  1  9
16 22 23 19 19 18 23 24 24 24 22 11 14  5  2 |  2  2  1  1  1  1 14  1  1  5 22
19 22 23 24 23 21 24 24 24 24 23 20 20 18  5 |  3  2  1  1  1 11 22  3  2 18 22
22 23 23 24 24 24 24 24 24 24 24 24 22 18    | 11  3  2  3 14 14  9  3 14 24 24
23 22 24 24 23 24 24 24 24 24 24 24 24  7    |  5  5  5  3  7  4  1  1  9 24 24
24 24 24 24 23 24 24 24 24 24 24 24 24 14    |  1  1  1  1  1  1  1  1  9 24 24
```

Tammie is a lovely, energetic & wildly creative woman! I thought quilted photography would be intense and difficult, but with amazing results.....only half of that is true, her technique is simple, clear and it does yield amazing results!
Alexis Durham
Manhattan Beach, CA

I loved the challenge of the quilt & how easy and quick it was. I love the surprise and comments when people walk into my house and see the quilted photo on the wall.
Cindy Plehn
Los Angeles, CA

Quilting Adds Texture And Beauty

In this chapter

❖ The Quilting Adds Another Layer Of Interest
❖ What Thread To Use?
❖ Free Motion Quilting
❖ Use Your Embroidery Machine For Quilting

The Quilting Adds Another Layer of Interest

The stitching you choose for your quilted art is a layer of texture.The texture is created by the pattern you stitch. If you compare the quilted photos to a panting, I think of the quilting as the brush strokes.

I will give you some of my ideas about quilting in this chapter. The stitching is also a layer of subtle color, bold contrasting color, or shine. You add this color or shine with the thread you use.

What Thread To Use?

I am in love with variegated threads! They come in 100% cotton, rayons, polyester and metallic. I use them all for different purposes, and I may even use more than one type in the same quilt. For example, I might use a metallic thread for the light areas of the quilt and a cotton or rayon for the darker areas. I like a lot of stitching and the variegated threads creates a more interesting line. A solid color thread would be

much to strong and would draw attention away from the image, but the change in the variegated colors keeps your eyes moving around the quilt. It really is a good idea to choose your thread at the beginning of the project. This way you can use the colors in your thread to help you pick your fabrics and also use it to stitch the quilt.

Free Motion Quilting

Free motion quilting can be either free form or you can follow a pattern. Sometimes I just doodle with my sewing machine, and it all just seems to look good in the end. The key is to just get the same amount of stitching over the whole surface.

A sample of some all over patterns are a stipple pattern,or a simple all over rounded zig-zag. If you are afraid of free motion you can also try a simple grid pattern. A grid pattern might look very interesting over your twisted squares. See page 42.

You can also try following the contours of your image. If your photo is of a face, your stitching will be a hint of the image when viewing from close up.

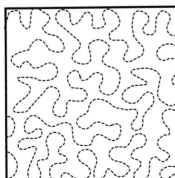

Stipple Quilting Pattern

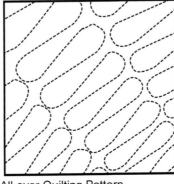

All over Quilting Pattern

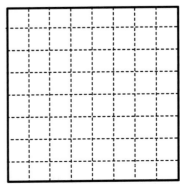

Simple Grid Quilting Pattern

To do free motion quilting, you will need to drop the feed dogs of your machine and move the fabric with your hands in any direction you like. The speed in which you move the fabric will determine the stitch length and the design. Practicing will make you more comfortable with free motion quilting.

Free motion can be very simple graphic shapes. The shapes don't have to be perfect, they just have to follow a general shape or pattern. I really like these gently curving vertical lines. Imagine how this would look with metallic threads!

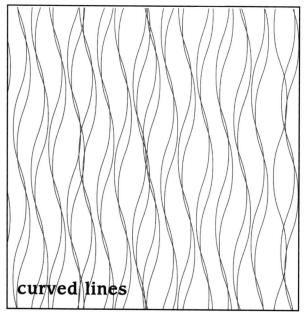

curved lines

Turn the quilt 90 degrees and continue stitching the curved lines to create a grid as shown. in the next column.

Try making these gently curving lines with a double or triple needle. The effect will be almost like calligraphy.

Another good free motion effect can be created by changing the stitch setting on your machine to the stretch zig zag stitch. The needle

will move back and forth as you move the quilt.

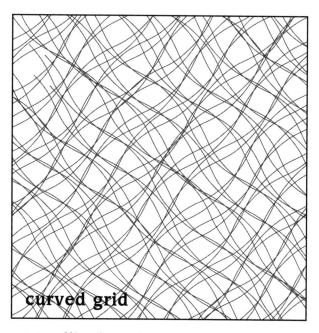

curved grid

Metallic threads are so beautiful, but can be difficult to work with because they are more fragile then other threads. Here are a few tips to keep the threads from breaking so often. The first thing is to use a vertical thread holder for your spool, second use a topstitch or metallic needle and thirdly if you are still having a problem, spray the spool with silicone spray to lubricate the thread and reduce friction.

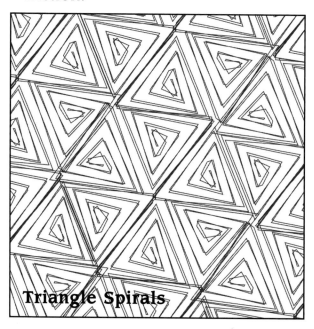

Triangle Spirals

An example of an easy free motion pattern are these triangle spirals. Remember perfection is not required. Just keep making triangles.

Try this basket weave pattern by alternating the direction of your quilting as shown above.

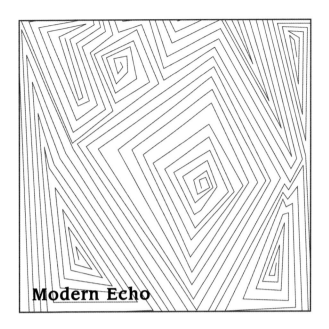

Modern Echo

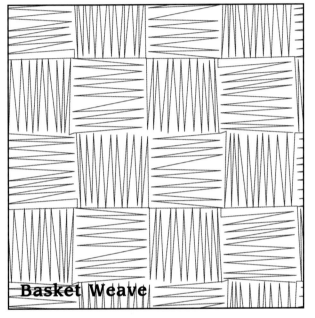

Basket Weave

This basket weave and the spiral triangle pattern is easier to do if you mark the rows of stitching with chalk or quilters tape as a guide before you start stitching.

One last easy idea I have for you to try is what I call "Modern Echo"stitching. You will start some place in the middle of the quilt and stitch around, and around, 1/4"or 1/8" away from the last stitching line. Fill in the open spaces until the whole quilt top has a cool,modern, but easy to do quilting design.

Use Your Embroidery Machine For Quilting

Have you ever thought of using your fancy embroidery machine for quilting? You can use your embroidery machine to create any of the designs I have described in the free motion section, but I prefer making design that are very hard to do with free motion. I used this perfect spiral for my ballerina quilt and it is fantastic! I overlapped the spirals all over the quilt and this would have been impossible to do with free motion quilting.

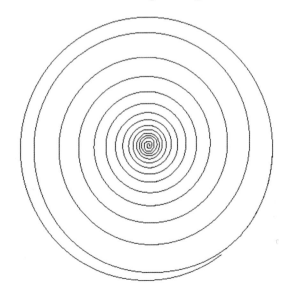

Here is another spiral design that you could make with an embroidery machine, but it would be very difficult to do with free motion.

To make all over quilting designs with your quilting machine, you have to understand how to create a repeat. A repeat is a small section of a pattern that makes a larger pattern when put together.

If you have digitizing software, and you understand repeats, you can make any simple or complex design into a quilting pattern.

Quilting with an embroidery machine is difficult to do on a large quilt. It is better suited for smaller quilts. This is because home embroidery machines don't have big openings, and the whole quilt will have to fit into the opening. Note that you will also have to hoop the quilt every time you want to stitch the pattern, this is another reason to use these techniques for smaller wall quilts.

Understanding Repeats

This next illustration is and example of a repeat. This is the smaller section of the overall pattern that is shown in the following illustration. Making a repeat for stitching requires that you start and stop at the same place so that you have a way to match the pattern. When you place the repeats next to each other, the starting and stopping point are in the exact same place.

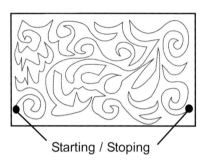

Starting / Stoping

A good source for quilting patterns is tessellations. These are interlocking shapes that can be simple or complex. M.C. Escher made very famous tessellations of lizards that would be fun to do in a quilt.

There are many books about M.C. Escher and tessellation , go to my website to see a list of books that have inspired me.

This next pattern is an advanced pattern you could digitize and quilt.
It is also inspired by M.C. Escher. The pattern is a complete block, and when the blocks are combined, the stitching almost seems to move when you look at it. I hope you have been inspired by this chapter.

With a single class, I was able to complete quilts with the unquestionable likeness of Rosa Parks and Rev. Martin Luther King Jr. They have been greeted with rave reviews. Who would have thought that a detailed portrait could be easily created by organizing fabrics and scraps. Following her simple rules, allows you to have tremendous results.
Sidney Hurd
Los Angeles, CA

Tammie, I did enjoy your class very much.. I was a little apprehensive at first, but the more I worked on it and then started sewing, it all came into place. My husband couldn't believe what he was seeing! Anyone that comes over keep asking "How did you do that?!"
Peggy Fullmer
Anaheim, CA

Finishing Your Quilted Art

In this chapter

- ❖ Completing The Project
- ❖ Trimming The Quilt
- ❖ Adding Borders
- ❖ Quilting Suggestions
- ❖ Bindings
- ❖ How To Display A Quilted Photo

Completing the project

Even though you have made your amazing photographic quilt top, the project is not complete until you have made it suitable for display. There are many ways you can finish your quilt top. I will discuss each of the available options in this chapter. The options range from borders, to bindings, to stretching your quilt top like a canvas!

Trimming The Quilt

If you have fused your pieces perfectly inside the lines, your quilt will finish with perfectly straight edges and squared corners. However this never happens and it is o.k. if your quilt is not perfect, you can trim the edges.

If you want to add a border to frame your quilt, trim the edges with your rotary cutter first. If you are just adding a binding to finish your quilt, then wait to trim the edges after stitching the layers of your quilt. Trimming will make sure that your quilt hangs straight when displayed on a wall.

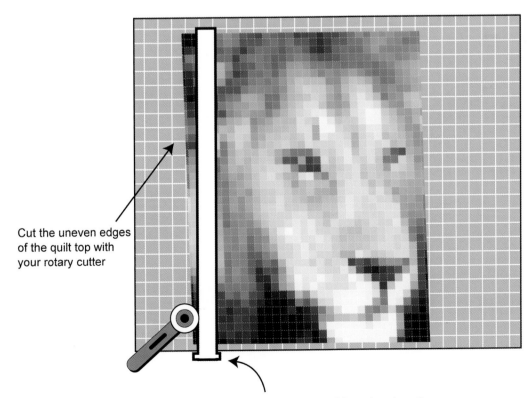

Cut the uneven edges of the quilt top with your rotary cutter

Slide the lip of the ruler along the edge of the mat to cut stright lines.

Adding Borders

A border is a straight strip of fabric sewn around the edges of your quilt to finish it.

A border can make your photo quilt even more beautiful but borders also have a practical purpose. Adding a border will make the edges of the quilt perfectly straight, and the corners will be perfectly squared. The border will make the quilted photo hang perfectly straight on the wall without any wavy edges. Another added bonus is the border will increase the size of the quilt and provide another place to put decorative quilting.

Adding a border is a decision you will make after you see the finished quilt top. You can add one or two borders or have no border at all.

When you think about adding borders to your quilted photos, you can pretend you are adding a matting and frame. Pay attention to the way paper photographs are framed. Also look at how paintings and other works of art are finished. Notice how the colors relate to the art work, and pay close attention to the proportion of the border in relation to the art work.

There are two types of borders, straight cut borders and mitered borders. I will explain both types.

To add a border, the first step is to measure at the center of the quilt in both directions. Be sure to measure in

Diagram A - Straight Border

Diagram B - Mitered Border

the center of the quilt
because the edges of the quilt are probably stretched and are not accurate. The center measurements will determine what length to cut the border strips. Cut the borders strips across the width of the fabric.

Straight border

A straight border has straight seams on the corners. See diagram A on page 54. To add a straight border, the first step is to measure the center of the quilt horizontally. Cut two border strips this exact length. Stitch the borders to the sides of the quilt, easing the quilt top to match the border if it is necessary.

Next measure the center of the quilt in the vertical direction including the border that you just applied. Cut two border strips that exact length. Stitch the border to the quilt, easing the two together if it is necessary. If you want a second straight border, repeat this process.

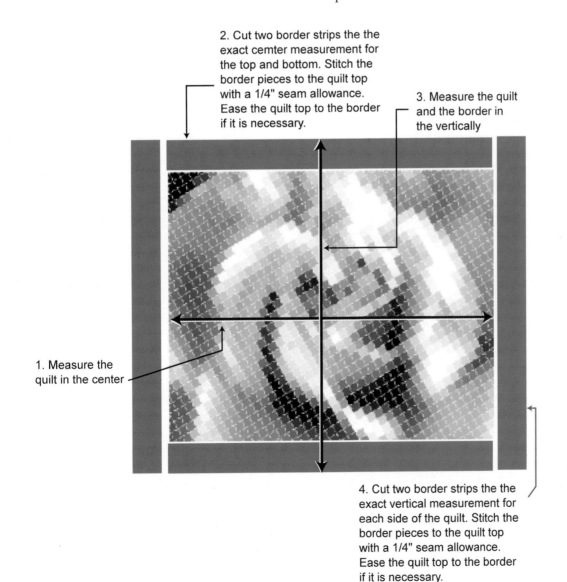

2. Cut two border strips the the exact cemter measurement for the top and bottom. Stitch the border pieces to the quilt top with a 1/4" seam allowance. Ease the quilt top to the border if it is necessary.

3. Measure the quilt and the border in the vertically

1. Measure the quilt in the center

4. Cut two border strips the the exact vertical measurement for each side of the quilt. Stitch the border pieces to the quilt top with a 1/4" seam allowance. Ease the quilt top to the border if it is necessary.

Mitered border

A mitered border is a border with diagonal seam on the corners. See diagram B on page 54.

To add a mitered border, first measure the center of the quilt in the vertical direction. Next measure the width of the border. Now cut two border strips the vertical length + the width of the border times 2. Mark the width of the border on each end of the border pieces. Cut the corners as shown in the diagram below. Cut from the outside corner, down to the border marks. Stitch the border pieces to the sides of the quilt, easing the quilt into the border if it is necessary. Stop your stitching ¼" from the edge. Repeat these steps for the horizontal edges of the quilt top.

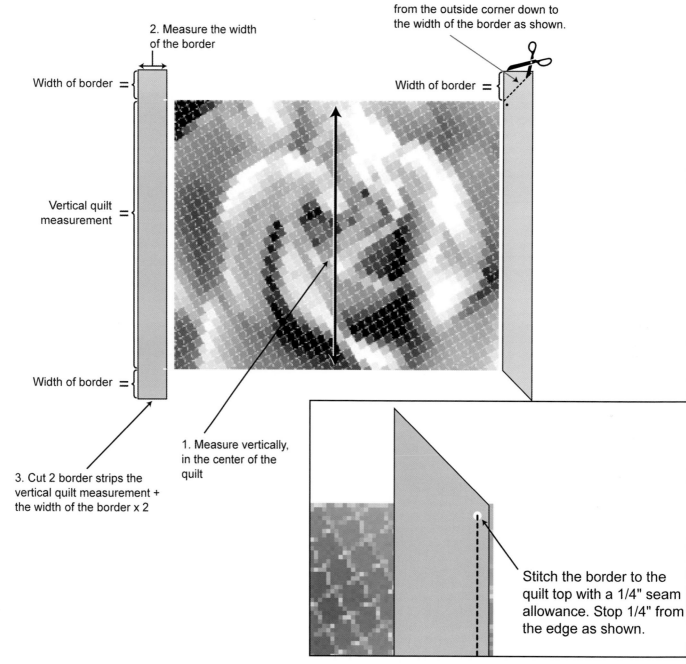

2. Measure the width of the border

Width of border =

Width of border =

Vertical quilt measurement =

Width of border =

3. Cut 2 border strips the vertical quilt measurement + the width of the border x 2

1. Measure vertically, in the center of the quilt

4. Cut the corners of the border from the outside corner down to the width of the border as shown.

Width of border =

Stitch the border to the quilt top with a 1/4" seam allowance. Stop 1/4" from the edge as shown.

To Create The Corner Seams
Fold the quilt in half diagonally so that the ends of the border meet. Stitch the corner seams with ¼" seam allowances. Repeat this step for all four corners.

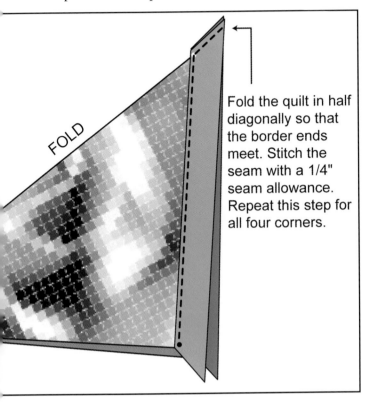

FOLD

Fold the quilt in half diagonally so that the border ends meet. Stitch the seam with a 1/4" seam allowance. Repeat this step for all four corners.

Batting And Backing

You can choose any backing fabric because the back of the quilt does not show. However I always use one of the fabrics that were used on the front of the quilt.

If your quilt top is larger than the width of the backing fabric, you will have to stitch two pieces of the backing fabric together to cover the back of the quilt. Remember to iron the backing seam open if a seam is required for your backing.

To sign your quilt, you can sign directly on the backing with a permanent pigment ink pen if you use a light colored fabric, or you can create an embroidered signature. You can also choose to apply a label to the back of the quilt.

The batting you use between the quilt top and the backing is again a matter of your preference. Batting is sold in standard bedding sizes as well as by the yard. Cotton battings are flatter when they are finished than polyester battings, but polyester and cotton blends are a good option as well. I usually use 100% cotton batting for my quilted photos. You can find batting in fabric and quilt stores.

Basting
Basting is a temporary bond that holds the quilt top, batting and backing together. Basting also assures that you will not have tucks or folds on the backing when you stich through your quilt sandwich.

You can baste the quilt sandwich by hand with a running stitch as shown in example A on page 58.

My favorite way to baste is to use an adhesive basting spray. Spray the adhesive between each layer of the quilt and the layers will hold together for the quilting process.

Basting stitched
through the
quilt sandwich

Quilt Top

Backing

Batting

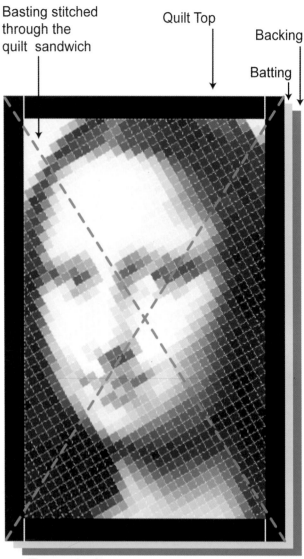

Example A

Quilting Suggestion

Try a stipple pattern. This is a
continuous curving stitch that never
crosses over itself. To create this pattern
beautifully, it takes practice but it is an
excellent quilting pattern to use for any
quilted photo project. Use a free motion
quilting foot (with your sewing
machine's feed dogs down) to create an
all over stipple pattern. Read Chapter 5
for more quilting ideas.

Simple Grid Pattern
The simple grid is the easiest all over
pattern for a quilted photo project. This
pattern is vertical and horizontal lines of
stitching arranged in a grid pattern.
This pattern is easy to make if you
create temporary guide lines to follow
with chalk or quilters tape. Use a walk-
ing foot to create the simple grid
pattern.

Bindings

After the quilting is finished, you still
need to finish the edges. You will finish
the edges with a binding and I will show
you how to make two different types.

The first type of binding is a classic
binding and the second type is an
invisible binding.

Classic Binding
A classic binding will make a ¼" edge
around the outside of the quilt. To make
a classic binding, the first thing you will
do is cut strips 1½" wide. Cut the strips
across the width of the fabric. Stitch the
strips together to form one long strip as
shown in diagram A.

Diagram A

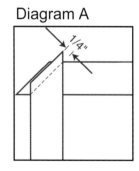

Fold the binding strip in half the long
way, and then place the binding on the

front of the quilt with the raw edges together. Stitch the binding with a ¼" seam allowance as shown in diagram B.

Diagram B

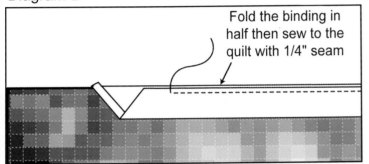

Fold the binding in half then sew to the quilt with 1/4" seam

shown. Pin the fold in place and stitch the next side of the binding. You can begin stitching from the corner edge.

Diagram E

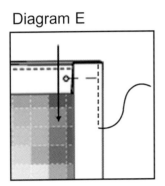

To continue the binding around the corner, stop stitching ¼" from the edge.

Diagram C

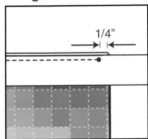

1/4"

Fold the binding upward, creating an angled corner as shown in diagram D.

Diagram D

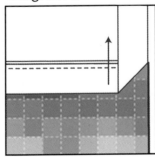

Then fold the binding back downward (creating a squared corner), leaving a fold of fabric as

The next step is to wrap the binding around the quilt edge, then over to the back as shown in diagram F. The last step is to stitch the edge of the binding in place with a small whipstitch.

Diagram F

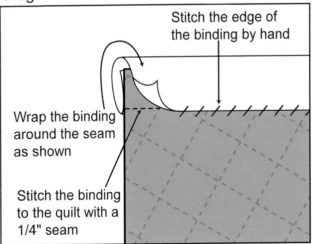

Stitch the edge of the binding by hand

Wrap the binding around the seam as shown

Stitch the binding to the quilt with a 1/4" seam

Invisible Binding

An invisible binding will not show at all when viewing the quilt from the front. To make an invisible binding, the first thing you will do is cut strips 1½" wide. Fold the binding strip in half, and then place the binding on the front of the quilt with the raw edges together. Stitch the binding with a ¼" seam allowance as shown in diagram B on page 59.

After stitching the binding all the way around the quilt, fold the binding and the seam upward, and away from the quilt. Stitch the binding 1/8" away from the seam as shown in the diagram below. This stitch will force the binding and the seam allowance to roll towards the backside of the quilt.

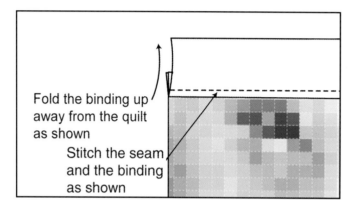

Fold the binding up away from the quilt as shown

Stitch the seam and the binding as shown

The last step is to stitch the edge of the binding in place with a small whipstitch.

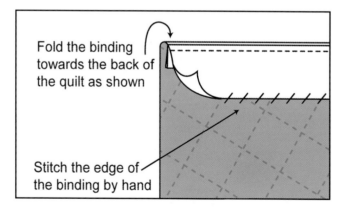

Fold the binding towards the back of the quilt as shown

Stitch the edge of the binding by hand

How To Display A Quilted Photo

When you prepare to display your quilt, you first need to think about how to care for the quilt. The most important thing you can do to preserve the quilt is to use UV protection spray. This spray will act just like a sunscreen and protect the fabrics from fading and sun damage.

Since these quilts are intended to be art that is hung on a wall, you should not have to worry about the quilts getting dirty. However you will need to remove dust from time to time if they are not framed behind glass. To remove the dust, just put the quilt in a clothes dryer for 10 minutes. The dryer will remove the dust without damaging the quilt.

After you have learned how to care for your quilt, you must decide how you will display it. The most obvious way to display your quilt is to have it framed professionally.

Another way you can display the quilt is to stretch it over a blank canvas. If you want to stretch it on a canvas you will not need to add a backing, batting or a binding. Center it over the canvas, then use a staple gun to secure the quilt top to the wooden frame of the canvas.

The way that I prefer to display my quilts is to add a sleeve to the back of the quilt as shown in the diagram on the next page. To add a sleeve, just make a 4" fabric tube the width of the quilt, then hand stitch it to the top of the quilt on both sides of the tube. To hang the quilt you will need a cafe curtain rod. Apply the curtain rod to the wall according to the manufacturer's instructions. Pull the curtain rod through the sleeve to hang the quilt. You can buy cafe curtain rods at any hardware store.

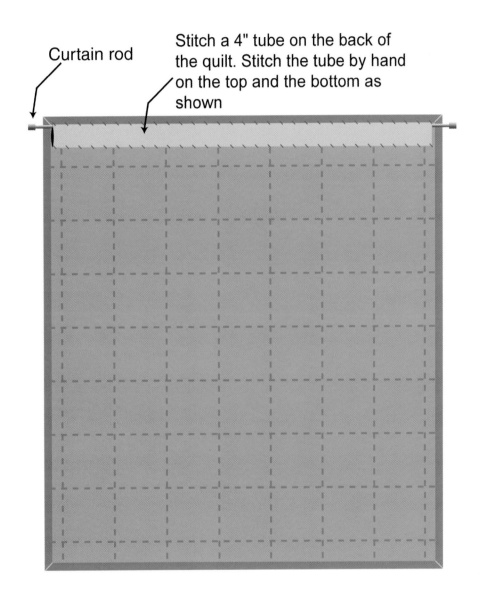

Curtain rod

Stitch a 4" tube on the back of the quilt. Stitch the tube by hand on the top and the bottom as shown

I've been quilting for 3 years and have never seen anything like your quilts, and I just had to take your class! It looked difficult but in fact is so easy and fun!!It was like paint by number but with fabric. Thanks for bringing this technique to us.
Debbie Sparr
Los Angeles, CA

I learned so much about the color value of fabrics! I now use this knowledge on other quilt blocks and wearable art. What a valuable addition to my quilting education! Thank You
Annette Berry
Los Angeles, CA

Quilted Photo Xpress 1.0

In this chapter

❖ Program User's Guide
❖ Program Tools
❖ Using The Program Tools
❖ Reading The Pattern
❖ How To Use The Grid Guide
❖ Finding The Values Of Your Fabrics

Program User's Guide

System Requirements

1. Microsoft Windows 95 or later
2. 90 MHz processor
3. 16 MB RAM
4. 32-bit color is a system requirement
5. A way to get photos into your computer(Photo processing CD, Scanner, digital camera, etc.)

If the Processed Photo does not display correctly within the program window, your display settings are set to either 16 or 256 colors. For the program to work properly, you must be able to display 32bit true color or greater. This is how to change your display settings: click Start->Control Panel, then double-click Display->Settings. Under "Colors," you need to select 32bit true color or greater.

Download Software

To download the software you must have internet access.
Go to this address:
www.quiltedphoto.com/QPX1
If you want Quilted Photo Xpress 1.0 on CD-Rom, read chapter 8 to find out how to get it.

Installation

1. Double click file: "Setup.exe".
2. Follow the installer's on-screen instructions.

Program Tools

A. Original Photo Display

This is the display of the original Photograph

B. Processed Photograph.

The processed photo changes as you change the settings below.

C. Detail Slider Bar.

As you move the selector, you will dynamically see the processed photo change.

D. Photo Detail Information Box

See how many pieces your quilt will have with the the current photo detail slider bar settings.

E. Number Of Fabrics selector Bar.

Slide the bar to the right to increase the number of fabrics or to the left to decrease. You will be able to dynamically see how the number of fabrics

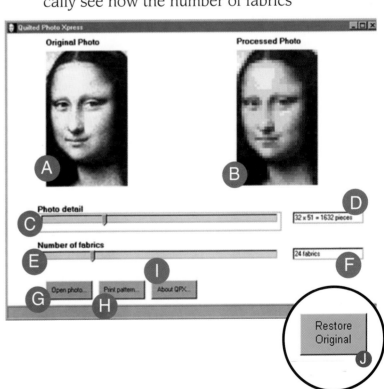

change the processed photo.

F. Number Of Fabrics Information Box.
This displays the number of fabrics with the the current number of fabrics slider bar setting.

G. Open Photo Button
Click this button to choose your own photos. You can use the following image formats: Bmp, jpeg and wmf

H. Print Pattern
Click this button to print your quilted photo pattern.

I. About QPX
Click this button for information about Mosaic Quilt Studio, and the software.

J. Selection Tool
You can also select a smaller area of your photo with the selection tool. You can use it by putting you cursor over your original photograph and holding down your left mouse button. Drag the mouse until the area you want as you pattern is selected. Let go of the left mouse button and process the photo with the other tools. When you select an area of the photo a button called "Restore" will appear. This button will restore the photo back to normal.

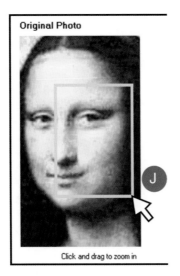

Original Photo

J

Click and drag to zoom in

Using The Program Tools

How Many Fabric Squares
The answer to this question depends on how much detail is in the image. If the image has a lot of small details then you will have to use more fabric squares to see the details clearly. If you decide to use to few squares, the image will look blurry. For a close-up image of a face, 1000 to 1600 squares is enough to see the image clearly, but for a dollar bill or a building, the small details may dictate 3000 -4000 pieces.

Photograph with lots of small details

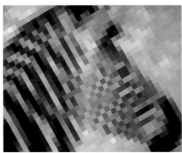

1112 squares = Lost details

3424 squares = Clear details

Straight Or Angled Grid

Your choice about what grid to use is just a matter of what you like most. The straight grid and the angled grid work equally well. If you want to make a photo with an angled grid you will need to turn the photo on and angle with a photo editing software or you can simply turn the photo on an angle when you scan it into your computer.

Making a pattern on the angle is not required for any of the techniques in this book but it can make your quilted photo more interesting. If you want to turn your photo on an angle, my suggestion is that you place the photo on a very dark or a white sheet of paper while scanning. This is so that you can tell which squares of the pattern are the background and not include them in your quilt.

techniques in this book, disregard the finished sized information) The pattern also includes the number of fabric pieces needed for each fabric you choose.

Note: the fabrics choices are organized from light to dark with #1 being the lightest and the highest number being the darkest. The last and most important part of the pattern is the pattern grid. It contains all of the numbered boxes that will create your photographic quilt. On each page you will find row and column information so that you can tape the complete pattern together as shown in this diagram.

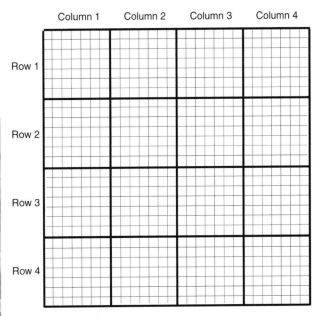

Straight Grid   Angled Grid

Reading The Pattern

The pattern printout includes your photo, the file name, the number of squares in your pattern, the number of fabrics you have chosen and four options for the finished quilt size. These sizes refer to the technique in my first book"Simply Amazing Quilted Photography".(If you will be using the

Fabric Requirement Chart

This chart will help you approximate the amount of fabric you will need. It tells

	1/16th yard	1/8th yard	1/4 yard	1/2 yard
1" squares	94	188	376	752
1 1/4" squares	55	110	220	440
1 1/2" squares	46	92	184	368
2" squares	23	46	92	184

the amount of squares you can cut out of 1/16th, 1/8th, 1/4 and 1/2 yard. These estimates are only for squares, but you will be able to get an idea of what you will need for other shapes as well.

The Color Palette

You will notice that the Color Palette is always arranged in order, with #1 being the lightest color and #24 being the darkest.

The Pattern Grid

The last and most important part of the pattern is the Pattern Grid. Each Pattern Grid contains numbered squares that correspond with your sorted and numbered fabrics.

How To Use The Grid Guide

The grid guide is a printed grid. To use the grid guide, place it under the fusible interfacing (adhesive side facing up) as a guide for arranging the fabric swatches.

Transfer the numbers from the Pattern Grid to the Grid Guide. Use a soft pencil to write the numbers into the grid (3B soft pencil). The soft lead is dark enough to see through the interfacing and it is easy to erase.

Place grid guide on the table

8	4	2	4	9	5	3	9	3	2	11	4	3	4
5	8	4	2	4	9	5	3	9	3	2	11	4	3
4	2	4	9	5	3	9	3	2	11	4	3	1	1
8	4	2	4	9	5	3	9	3	2	11	4	3	4
5	8	4	2	4	9	5	3	9	3	2	11	4	3
4	2	4	9	5	3	9	3	2	11	4	3	1	1
8	4	2	4	9	5	3	9	3	2	11	4	3	4
5	8	4	2	4	9	5	3	9	3	2	11	4	3
4	2	4	9	5	3	9	3	2	11	4	3	1	1
8	4	2	4	9	5	3	9	3	2	11	4	3	4

Place fusible interfacing on top of the grid guide

If the pattern has a straight grid then put the guide under the interfacing the same way it appears. If you made your pattern on an angle then use the following instructions for positioning the grid guide.

You will need a quilting ruler that has a 30 degree or a 60 degree mark on it. Line up the 30 or 60 degree angle with the straight edge of the interfacing as shown in the diagram A.

Mark a 30 degree line as shown in the diagram. Next you will line up the edge of the grid with the angled line you have drawn (diagram B).

If you made your pattern on an angle other than 30 or 60 degree, then match the angle of your pattern for this step.

Grid Guide

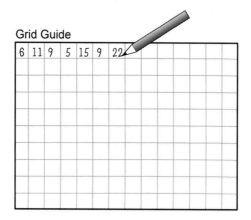

6	11	9	5	15	9	22				

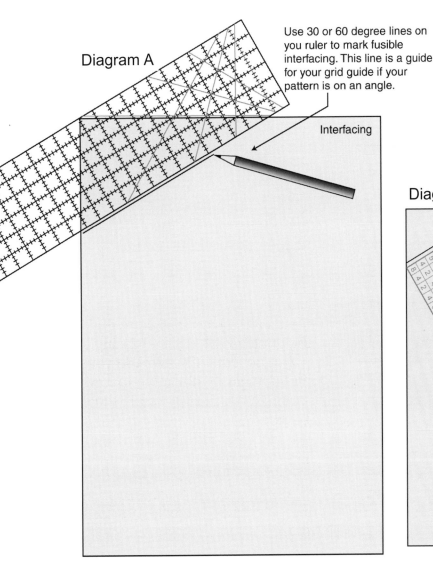

Diagram A

Use 30 or 60 degree lines on you ruler to mark fusible interfacing. This line is a guide for your grid guide if your pattern is on an angle.

Interfacing

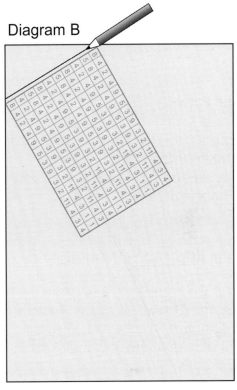

Diagram B

Finding The Values Of Your Fabrics

I discussed finding the values of your fabrics and taught you how to use a photocopy machine to see the values in chapter 2, but using the software is much easier. Cut a 1", square piece of the fabrics to make your quilted photo. (remember the 888 rule in chapter 2).Your goal is to have colored fabrics that represent shades from light to dark.

Place the squares on the form on page 69. Please cut the squares 1" so that the entire width of the page is covered by fabric. If your fabric pieces are smaller than 1", the white spaces between the squares will make your results confusing.It is also important to make all of your fabrics fit on the page at one time.

Scan your form into your computer and save the image of your fabrics as a jpeg file. Open your file in the Quilted Photo Xpress 1.0 *Original Photo Display* window. Now move the *Number Of Fabrics selector Bar* to match the number of fabrics on your form.

Next move the *Photo Detail Slider* all the way to the left, until the number it says matches the fabrics across the top row.

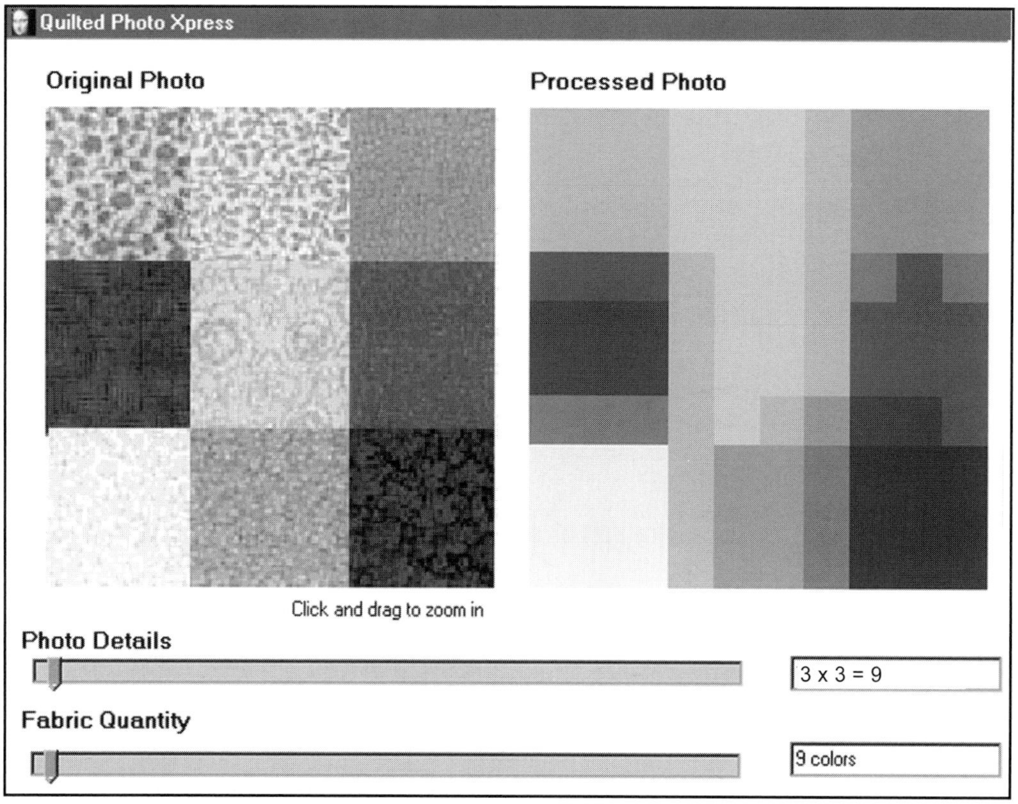

Now use the selection tool to only select the fabrics, and none of the surrounding form as shown in the diagram above.

The last thing to do is print the pattern. You will ignore everything except the grid of numbers. The grid will tell you what value each of the swatches are. The pattern will look something like the diagram below.

If two of your swatches have the same color value, then make your decision by looking at the fabrics to determine the value, or choose another fabric and start the process over again.

That is all you need to know to use Quilted Photo Xpress 1.0.

Quilted Photo Xpress 2.0 is available with a realistic color option. With this option, the program will choose the fabric colors for you! Quilted Photo Xpress 2.0 will also print your

3	2	5
7	2	5
1	4	9

grid in full size, just like a Grid Guide with the numbers already in it! Go to chapter 8 to learn more about Quilted Photo Xpress 2.0.

Quilted Photo Xpress / Color Value Swatch Form

Attach Fabric Swatch Here	Attach Fabric Swatch Here	Attach Fabric Swatch Here	Attach Fabric Swatch Here	Attach Fabric Swatch Here	Attach Fabric Swatch Here
Attach Fabric Swatch Here	Attach Fabric Swatch Here	Attach Fabric Swatch Here	Attach Fabric Swatch Here	Attach Fabric Swatch Here	Attach Fabric Swatch Here
Attach Fabric Swatch Here	Attach Fabric Swatch Here	Attach Fabric Swatch Here	Attach Fabric Swatch Here	Attach Fabric Swatch Here	Attach Fabric Swatch Here

We enjoyed your class very much. You made it so easy. We had so many great comments on the quilts we made. We are planning on making 6 more!
Martha Christensen & Cora Hall
Carson, CA

Dear Tammie,
I am thankful that your class was available. After ten years, it took my quilting to a higher level!
Ozellia Crawford
Los Angeles, CA

Tools And Materials You Will Need

Quilted Photo Xpress 2.0 Software

This software is amazing! It will let you make a pattern from your own photos.
You will have these options:
- Numbers Of Fabrics
- Number Of Pieces
- Realistic Color Palette
- Easily Adjust The Color Balance Of Photos
- Print Your Color Palette For Shopping
- Prints full sized patterns. Just like a grid guide with the numbers printed in the squares for you.

Quilted Photo Xpress 2.0 Upgrade

If you bought the 1.0 version of the software, you are eligible for an upgrade to the 2.0 version. To get this upgrade, you must send the paper cover as proof of purchase with your order.

Quilted Photo Xpress 1.0/Limited Edition on Cd-Rom

You can get this software for free if you download it from the website at:
www.quiltedphoto.com/QPX1
You can also purchase this software on CD-rom.

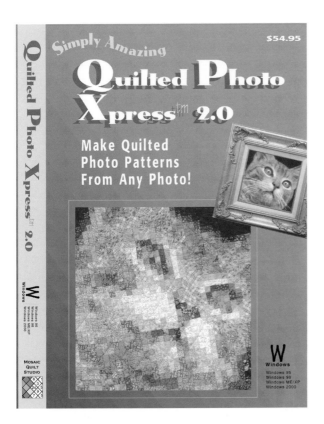

Extra Wide Fusible Web Packages

Fusible web is necessary for all of the techniques in this book. You will fuse it to the back of all your fabric. Fusible web is applied with an iron and non-stick surface. Each package comes with a bonus 20″ x 20″ sheet of two sided, non-stick paper. This non-stick paper can be used over and over, with any fusible web. The web is 60″ wide and comes in 2 yard packages

Extra Wide Fusible Tricot Packages

Fusible tricot is a necessary item you will need to create your photo quilt. You will use it to fuse the fabric pieces together before using the quick sewing techniques (see chapter4). This tricot is used along with grid guides. This tricot is what I use for my Quilted Photos. The tricot is very soft and won't stiffen your quilt. It is 60″ wide and comes in 2 yard packages

Grid Guides

A grid guide is a full sized grid that is printed on paper. The grid guide is placed under your fusible interfacing or tricot, as a guide for placing your fabric pieces. A grid guide can be used over and over to create photo quilts. You can even tape several grid guides together to make a big guide. You will get one free grid guide with every order. Each Grid Guide measures 24″ x 36″ and you can choose 11/4″, 11/2″, 1″ or 3/4″ squares Comes 4 per package.

Fabric Organizer Box

The best way that I have found to organize the fabric squares is to use this organizer case. It has 24 compartments of the perfect size. Look at chapter 2 to see just how important this simple tool is.

Distance Viewer

This is my favorite tool! This small scope will let you quickly see the photographic image in your quilt just by looking through it. It is useful while you are working on the quilt, and it is fun to use after the quilt is finished. Each time I work on a new quilt, I think to myself "It didn't work this time", when I look at the quilt through the distance viewer, the image just pops out at me! If you plan to make any of these quilts as gifts, you must give them a distance viewer too! Made of solid brass.

Non-Stick Paper

You can order more of this great non-stick paper. I cover my whole ironing surface with this two sided non-stick paper. I use it for applying fusible web to my fabrics. You can get a small piece when you order my extra wide fusible web, but you can also get a larger roll (20″ x 72″).

Silicone Spray

Silicone spray is used for lubricating delicate metallic threads. It will reduce friction and is an easy way to stop metallic threads from breaking so often. It is non-greasy, and won't stain your fabrics.

Fusible Web Spray

This is a fantastic time saver! you just spray the back of your fabrics, let dry for a few minutes, and your fabric is prepared for quilted photography! Read product instructions for the iron temperature to use. 8.5 oz. can

Ruler Handle

This handle has double suction cups that you attach to the top of any acrylic ruler. The handle will hold your ruler with securely and with ease while cutting. Protects hand and fingers from rotary cutter. Suction cups can be easily released by lifting edges of suction cups.

Ruler Guide

This guide is a lip that you can stick on to your acrylic ruler. It is repositionable and stable. It is great to use along with the ruler handle.

Basting Spray

You can baste the quilt layers together instantly with this spray. It is a repositionable, temporary bond between the layers of your quilt The spray will not gum your needle and washes out completely. It Is odorless and colorless.

UV Protection Spray

Quiltgard Fabric Protector with U.V. Sun Screen is an environ-mentally-safe protectant recom-mended for use on quilts. Will increase the ability of the fibers to repel liquids and retard fading when exposed to the sun. Each 11 oz. can protects up to 50 square feet of fabric.

Mini Iron

For the techniques taught in this book, I use this mini iron. It gives you control while fusing small pieces of fabric.

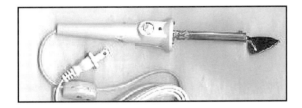

Simply Amazing Quilted Photography

This is the original book teaching my simple technique for Quilted Photography. It is a classic.

More Amazing Quilted Photography

Order another copy for your friends!

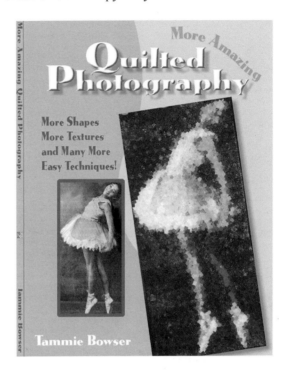

Go to the order form on page 80 to continue.

Quilted Photography is totally unique and exciting. It involves two things that makes me love quilting, it's looks hard but is really quite simple. And it is fun too!
Jan Emanuel
Pasadena, CA

I learned more about color value in the one day class than at Art School! Tammie's instructions were great! I watched my photo come to life in the class. I will treasure my quilt for a lifetime!
Darlen Lee
Acton, CA

My goal has been to teach you how to make your own Quilted Photos and to teach you more ways to do it. I hope you agree that I have reached my goal. I have explored threads and quilting, texture, shape color and photography in new ways. I have given you a limited version of my software and taught you to use it to make patterns as well as how to use it to determine the value of your fabrics.

I have enjoyed sharing my ideas, and my quilts with you. I would also like to see your Quilted Photos. Please send me pictures of your projects.

Send your photos to:
Mosaic Quilt Studio
917 Fremont PMB138
South Pasadena, California, 91030

Please sign my guest book located on my website, I will share my new techniques, offer my products at a discount, and even invite you you contribute to my next book! Sign the guest book today!

Thank you to P&B Textiles for the fabrics! The beautiful colors have inspired me to create these new techniques.

Thank you to Janome America for the fantastic sewing machines. The Memorycraft 10000 and the Quilters Companion 6260 have made my work more creative and enjoyable!

Thank you for your interest in "More Amazing Quilt Photography".

Tammie Bowser

Quilted Photography is just fabulous! Creating a quilt with your cherished photo on it is a great idea. My daughter Rosie (16 years old) and I have enjoyed making your quilts. It is something we enjoy doing together.
Kath Robi
Pasadena, CA

It was a fun experience to watch my photo "appear" as the fabric pieces were added!
Marcy Young
Sherman Oaks, CA

I began sewing at four years of age. With my natural talent for sewing I made my own clothing in jr. high and high school. I went on to fashion college (The Fashion Institute of Design and Merchandising). I studied fashion design, color theory and pattern making then graduated in 1985. My 17 year fashion career included positions as a fashion designer, production patternmaker and first patternmaker.

I also studied website design, graphic design and desktop publishing. My new computer knowledge combined perfectly with my design, fashion, and sewing knowledge. I went on to start a website called www.Ez-fit.com. This site makes custom sized clothing patterns for people who sew.

Throughout my busy careers, I held an interest in quilting but, never took the time to learn it. With lots of time at home after My daughter was born, in the fall of 2000, I began to read books about quilting. Quilting captivated me, and I began to focus my creativity towards it.

I made my first quilt as a gift for my mother in November of 2000. I taught myself how to quilt by reading books, and watching the HGTV series, "Simply Quilts". After making that first quilt, I wanted to design my own quilt patterns. One morning just a few weeks later, I woke up with the idea for Quilted Photos. My first thought was that it couldn't work, but I made the first quilted photo that very week. I was amazed at how stunning the results were, and am still amazed every time I complete a Quilted Photo.

I think my career paths, and collection of knowledge has given me this unique approach to quilting. I hope you enjoy this innovative quilting style as much as I do.

Look for Tammie on HGTV's "Simply Quilts" episode #819, Kaye Wood's show "Friends of Kaye" #K1404 on PBS.

Tammie is a lovely, energetic & wildly creative woman! I thought quilted photography would be intense and difficult, but with amazing results.....only half of that is true, her technique is simple, clear and it does yield amazing results!
Alexis Durham
Manhattan Beach, CA

For a long time I had been trying to introduce pictures into my quilts, so I learned different techniques to make memory quilts. It was OK for a while, but your Quilted Photography was what I was looking for! It is a real picture experience. I LOVE IT!
Francisca Reynoso
Valley Glen, CA

I Loved your class. I did a combination of my 2 grandchildren. Everyone loves it. I had a lot of enjoyment working on it.
Jo Ann Felter
Buena Park, CA

These quilts are extremely easy and fun to make! They make great gift quilts. The instructions are easy to follow and your class was a lot of fun! This is a great quilt for any beginner or advanced quilter!
Sue Vite